Red Riding Hood

Written by Ann Wade
Illustrated by Carla Daly

Collins *Educational*
An imprint of HarperCollins *Publishers*

Storyteller: When Red Riding Hood went to visit her grandmother her mother told her not to leave the path...

2

...but she left the path to pick flowers.

Her mother told her not to talk to strangers...

4

...but she talked to a wolf.

Her mother told her not to tell anyone where she was going...

...but she told the wolf that she was going to visit her grandmother. And this is what happened at Grandmother's cottage...

7

Red Riding Hood: Grandmother, Grandmother, are you there?
Wolf (*in a high voice*): Yes, my dear. Come right in.

Red Riding Hood: Oh, Grandmother, why are you tucked up in bed?
Wolf: I am not feeling very well, my dear.
Come a little closer.

9

Red Riding Hood: Oh, Grandmother, what big ears you have.

Wolf: All the better to hear you with, my dear.
Come a little closer.

Red Riding Hood: Oh, Grandmother, what big eyes you have.
Wolf: All the better to see you with, my dear.
Come a little closer.

Red Riding Hood: Oh, Grandmother, what big teeth you have.
Wolf: All the better to bite you with.

Red Riding Hood: Help! Help! Help!

Woodcutter (*enters and chases the wolf out*): Oh, no you don't, you wicked wolf.

Storyteller: Red Riding Hood found her grandmother tied up in the wardrobe and set her free. She told her grandmother what had happened and promised never to talk to strangers again.